The Way Into ...

The Way Into ... Series offers an accessible and highly usable "guided tour" c tory, and beliefs—in total, an introduction to Judaism that will enable you to under cred texts of the Jewish tradition.

Each volume is written by a leading contemporary scholar and teacher, and explores one key aspect of Judaism.

The Way Into ... enables all readers to achieve a real sense of Jewish cultural literacy through guided study.

Other volumes in the series

The Way Into Judaism and the Environment

By Jeremy Benstein, PhD

Explores the ways in which Judaism contributes to contemporary social-environmental issues, the extent to which Judaism is a part of the problem, and how it can be part of the solution.

6 x 9, 288 pp, Hardcover, ISBN-13: 978-1-58023-268-5
ISBN-10: 1-58023-268-X

The Way Into Varieties of Jewishness

By Sylvia Barack Fishman, PhD

Explores the religious and historical understanding of what it has meant to be Jewish from ancient times to the present controversy over "who is a Jew?"

6 x 9, 288 pp, Hardcover, ISBN-13: 978-1-58023-030-8
ISBN-10: 1-58023-030-X

The Way Into Torah

By Rabbi Norman J. Cohen, PhD

Explores the origins and development of Torah, why it should be studied, and how to do it.

6 x 9, 176 pp, Quality PB, ISBN-13: 978-1-58023-198-5
ISBN-10: 1-58023-198-5
Hardcover, ISBN-13: 978-1-58023-028-5
ISBN-10: 1-58023-028-8

The Way Into Encountering God in Judaism

By Rabbi Neil Gillman, PhD

Explores the many images of God in Jewish tradition, how they originated and what they can mean for you and your spiritual life.

6 x 9, 240 pp, Quality PB, ISBN-13: 978-1-58023-199-2
ISBN-10: 1-58023-199-3
Hardcover, ISBN-13: 978-1-58023-025-4
ISBN-10: 1-58023-025-3

The Way Into *Tikkun Olam* (Repairing the World)

By Rabbi Elliot N. Dorff, PhD

Learn the importance of justice, compassion, and social and familial harmony for both the individual and society in Jewish tradition.

6 x 9, 320 pp, Quality PB, ISBN-13: 978-1-58023-328-6
ISBN-10: 1-58023-328-7
Hardcover, ISBN-13: 978-1-58023-269-2
ISBN-10: 1-58023-269-8

The Way Into Jewish Mystical Tradition

By Rabbi Lawrence Kushner

Explores the concepts of Jewish mysticism, their religious and spiritual significance, and how they relate to our lives.

6 x 9, 224 pp, Quality PB, ISBN-13: 978-1-58023-200-5
ISBN-10: 1-58023-200-0
Hardcover, ISBN-13: 978-1-58023-029-2
ISBN-10: 1-58023-029-6

Contents

[Note: Each session relates to a chapter in *The Way Into Jewish Prayer* by Rabbi Lawrence A. Hoffman, PhD.]

The Way Into Jewish Prayer Teacher's Guide

2007 First Printing

ISBN-13: 978-1-58023-345-3 (pbk.)
ISBN-13: 978-1-68336-446-7 (hc)

First Edition

Manufactured in the United States of America

Published by Jewish Lights Publishing
www.jewishlights.com

Introduction

At some stage in our lives, most of us struggle with the question of prayer. What is prayer and what does it mean to us? What is the history of Jewish prayer? How does it function in our synagogues and homes? There is no simple answer. Jewish prayer requires us to think through each word we say at services, begs us to take natural wonders into account, and challenges us to embrace prayer at all times. Rabbi Lawrence Hoffman, author of *The Way Into Jewish Prayer,* has given us a great tool to help find the answers to these difficult questions. His book takes readers on a personal journey through prayer and what it means in our lives.

The Way Into Jewish Prayer Teacher's Guide is designed to help translate this spiritual journey into the classroom. It is written for adult education classes and uses a discussion format to spark intellectual thought and dialogue. The goal of the guide is to challenge students by bringing the big questions of the book into the classroom: the *why, how, where,* and *what* of prayer. This guide invites everyone to take a look inside and grapple with the tough choices of becoming a prayerful person.

The teacher's guide consists of six sessions, which coincide with each chapter of the book. In every session there are 3–4 activities from which a teacher can choose. Each activity should take 30 minutes to an hour depending on the level of discussion within the group. (Students are expected to read the appropriate chapter from the text prior to attending class.) At the beginning of each session there are a series of set induction questions and a key quotation from the chapter to help introduce the activities that follow. Teachers are encouraged to use these two prompts before any of the activities within the session. Activities with icons ✎ alert the teacher that advanced preparation is necessary for the activity, and you will need to plan accordingly. Each activity concludes with brief wrap-up text that is specific to the topic at hand.

The Way Into Jewish Prayer provides the necessary tools to become a prayerful person. In Rabbi Hoffman's words, "Becoming a prayerful person is about the choices we make" (p. 166). This guide will help students along that journey. When, for example, we choose to articulate our prayers either communally or individually, we increase the chance of living our lives the way we would like. "We can choose merely to hope to be good to others, or we can elect to pray about goodness and thereby become more likely to actually do the good that we intend" (p. 166).

Becoming a prayerful person takes work and dedication. It is filled with successes and failures, and requires us to interact both communally and individually with God. It encourages us to see the world and its creations through a new awe-inspiring lens. It challenges our comfort level, our fears, and reshapes our time. But even with all of that, the rewards of praying are everlasting. "We can live in homes with nothing that is sacred, true, and noble, or we can fill our lives with prayer and blessing at every turn" (p. 166).

"Finding the way into Jewish prayer can be the first step on a life-changing and life-enhancing journey" (p. 166).

A Note on Translation

Unless otherwise noted, the Bible translation I have used in this guide is from the Jewish Publication Society's translation of the *Tanakh* (1999).

God and the Jewish People: To Whom Jews Pray

Set Induction

Have students answer the following questions on a piece of paper:

1. What is prayer?
2. Do you believe your prayers are answered? If so, how do you know?
3. To whom do you pray?
4. Why pray?

Introduction to Lesson

"Prayer seems to presuppose the existence of a deity who listens to what we say, wants us to say it, and somehow responds. Prayer is not simply a question of what Jews say to God. It is also about the God who is at the other end, listening" (p. 2).

Activity 1
The Three Prayer Books

Materials

- *Copies of siddur, machzor,* and *haggadah*
- Copies of *The Way Into Jewish Prayer*

Procedure

1. Review the section on the three prayer books—the *siddur*, the *machzor,* and the *haggadah*—on pages 10–11 of *The Way Into Jewish Prayer.*
2. Pass out copies of each type of prayer book.
3. Ask students the following:
   a. What are the differences and similarities between the three prayer books?
   [*Teacher's Tip: There are countless similarities and differences among these three books. The simple difference is that they are used at different times of worship. The* siddur *for*

weekly and Shabbat prayer, the machzor *for holidays, and the* haggadah *for Passover. A similarity is that within each prayer service there is a set order to follow.]*

b. Prayer is done in a particular order. What are some examples of this from the three prayer books? Using these three prayer books, what are some examples of how prayer is performed in a particular order?

c. Are you more familiar with a particular prayer book? If so, which one and why?

d. How do you use prayer books in your life?

   i. Are they necessary for you? Why or why not?

   ii. Do you feel most comfortable when praying with or without them? Why?

Wrap-up

There are many opportunities in our lives to pray. Jewish tradition provides a number of prayer books that have been created for certain times of the week, month, and year. Within these various prayer books an order is followed. This allows for Jews all over the world to share prayers with similar components. By using prayer books, our prayer experience can be enhanced by the words of our tradition.

Activity 2
God Who Is Real

Materials

- Copies of *The Way Into Jewish Prayer*

Procedure

1. Ask for volunteers to read aloud the quotations on pages 15–16 of *The Way Into Jewish Prayer.*
2. Allow students time to reflect on them.
3. Ask students to choose the one that speaks to them the most and have them share their thoughts with the class.
4. Ask students:
   a. Why does this quotation speak to you?
   b. Did it change or add anything to the beliefs you had formulated prior to this class?
   c. Does this concept of prayer enter your daily life? If yes, when?

Wrap-up

Each person has a unique relationship to prayer. For some of us, prayer comes easily; for others, it is much more difficult. When we pray, we are given the opportunity to be awed by the world, our bodies, and God. By allowing ourselves to take in all of these mysteries, we experience something holy and profound.

Activity 3

Classical God Concepts

Materials

- Copies of Hand-out I: Three Classical God Concepts
- Marker
- Large piece of paper

Procedure

1. Read the definitions of the three classical God concepts—watchmaker, parent, omnipotent—and the text examples.
2. Ask students for their reactions to the text examples.
3. On a large piece of paper, draw the God concept sliding scale, found on Hand-out I. Ask the following:
   a. Where do you see yourself on the scale and why?
   b. Does this say anything about the way we communicate with God?
4. Ask students how their concept of God corresponds with how they pray.
5. Ask students if particular prayers speak to them because of the type of God they address.

Wrap-up

The God we believe in can take on different roles for each of us. For some, God functions in the world as a watchmaker. For others, God is a caring parent, or is all knowing and all powerful. There is no right or wrong answer. Talking about these definitions and reading texts that support them shapes our personal theology.

Hand-out I

Three Classical God Concepts

WATCHMAKER

The idea that God created the universe and set it in motion, just as a watchmaker makes a watch and sets it to run on its own. There is no need for the watchmaker to ever see the watch again, even if it breaks down. Some problems can be fixed by the owner of the watch, others require a watch repairperson. Likewise, some problems in the universe can be fixed by individuals, and others by organized religion.

> "And God created man in God's image, in the image of God the Divine created him; male and female God created them. God blessed them and God said to them, "'Be fertile and increase, fill the earth and master it; and rule the fish of the sea, the birds of the sky, and all the living things that creep on earth" (Gen. 1:27–28).

> "The Lord put out the Lord's hand and touched my mouth, and the Lord said to me: Herewith I put My words into your mouth. See, I appoint you this day over nations and kingdoms: to uproot and to pull down, to destroy and to overthrow, to build and to plant" (Jer. 1:9–10).

PARENT

The idea that God created and cares for the universe and all who dwell in it, just as a parent creates and cares for a child. The parent is very active in the child's life at the beginning, teaching and helping the child to do more and more on its own until the relationship is equalized in adulthood. Likewise, God was very active in the beginning stages of the universe (such as described in the Torah) and through Torah, enabled the universe to function on its own, turning to God only when in need of guidance.

> "And God continued, 'I have marked well the plight of My people in Egypt and have heeded their outcry because of their taskmasters; yes, I am mindful of their sufferings. I have come down to rescue them from the Egyptians and bring them out of that land to a good and spacious land'" (Exod. 3:7–8).

> "Our Father, our King, hear our voice. Our Father, our King, we have sinned against You. Our Father, our King, have compassion on us and on our children. Our Father, our King, make an end to sickness, war, and famine" (from *Avinu Malkeinu*).

OMNIPOTENT

The idea that God created everything; is all-knowing and all powerful; and continues to be the ultimate cause for everything. God's involvement with creation is ongoing and necessary. Nothing would or could happen without God.

> "The earth became corrupt before God; the earth was filled with lawlessness. When God saw how corrupt the earth was, for all flesh had corrupted its ways on earth, God said to Noah, 'I have decided to put an end to all flesh, for the earth is filled with lawlessness because of them: I am about to destroy them with the earth'" (Gen. 6:11–13).

> "If, then, you obey the commandments that I enjoin upon you this day, loving the Lord your God and serving God with all your heart and soul, I will grant the rain for your land in season, the early rain and the late" (Deut. 11:13–14).

God Concept Sliding Scale

Watchmaker — Parent — Omnipotent

◄————————————————————►

Note: If none of the above accurately describes your concept of God, name and describe an alternative that you find more compelling.

SESSION II

Prayer as Discipline and as Art: How Prayer Works

Set Induction

Have students answer the following questions on a piece of paper:

1. List what you know about the actual structure of prayer.
2. List what you know about the structure of the prayer book.
3. As Jews, where and when do we pray?
4. Where and when do you find it most comfortable to pray?

Introduction to Lesson

> "Prayer allows us to appreciate the universe, to express our hopes of what a better universe might be, ever to shout defiance when we see injustice occurring. Prayer is a way to elevate our thoughts to speech, and even to formulate better thoughts because of the power that speech has over the way we think. Because it draws on traditional language, it roots us in the history of our hallowed past, and because it is primarily communal, it overcomes loneliness by binding us to a worldwide community that dares to 'dream in league with God'" (p. 37).

Activity 1

The Pattern of Prayer

Advance Preparation

Teachers should take time prior to class to go through the prayer structure on pages 22–26 of *The Way Into Jewish Prayer* and study a prayer book to become familiar with what they will ask their students.

Materials

- Prayer books
- Paper
- Pencils/pens

- Copies of *The Way Into Jewish Prayer*
- Copies of the structure of the prayer service

Procedure

1. Ask students to list the top three things they learned from reading the section "The Pattern of Prayer" on pages 20–26 of *The Way Into Jewish Prayer.*
2. Pass out prayer books and sheets with the structure of the prayer service on them.
3. Go through the prayer book, identifying and making note of the structure while you do so.
4. Talk about the following questions with students:
   a. Does the structure work for you?
   b. Does it seem logical?
   c. Is a structure important to a prayer service?
   d. Have you ever felt that the structure of a prayer service evoked special feelings in you while you were praying?
   e. Have you ever felt that the structure gets in your way?

Wrap-up

Prayer comes with rules. There are fixed times to pray and a specific order of prayers. Each prayer component contributes to the prayer experience as a whole. By being aware of the components that make up a prayer service, we can augment whatever personal meaning we invest in prayer by appreciating the overarching themes and concerns that have been passed down by Jewish tradition.

Activity 2

The Three Places to Pray—The Synagogue, the Home and the Everyday World

Materials

- Copies of Hand-out II: A Story Based on an Anonymous Hasidic Tale
- Copies of *The Way Into Jewish Prayer*

Procedure

1. Pass out copies of Hand-out II: A Story Based on an Anonymous Hasidic Tale.
   Ask for a volunteer to read the story to the class, then ask the following questions:
   a. What does it mean to have a place to pray?
   b. Is it important to have somewhere that is comfortable for you to go to pray? If so, why? What advantage is that to you?
   c. Moshe found his place to pray in the woods. Do you have one?

2. Summarize for students the history behind prayer in the synagogue, the home, and our daily lives. See pages 26–32 of *The Way Into Jewish Prayer* for guidance and ask the following questions:
   a. Why is it important to have all three?
   b. What can we get from each that is different or similar?

Wrap-up

Being a prayerful person takes practice; there will not be immediate success. Judaism gives us particular places and opportunities to enter into prayer that allow prayer slowly to affect our daily lives. "Becoming a prayerful person is like becoming a marathon runner or a world-class chef. It takes regular practice. And it presupposes failures along the way to ultimate success" (p. 31).

Hand-out II

A Story Based on an Anonymous Hasidic Tale

There once was a small village. And in that village lived a man, Moshe, and a rabbi. Each morning Moshe would wake up, make breakfast, wash himself, and prepare to go out. And each morning he would leave his humble home and head into the woods that could be found on the edge of the village. He wandered for hours in those woods, never seeing another soul and only returned in time to go to work. The rabbi started to take notice of Moshe. After about two weeks the rabbi decided one evening to go to Moshe's home and ask him about his daily adventures. Moshe welcomed the rabbi and made some tea. They entered into conversation and right before the rabbi was about to take his leave, he said to Moshe, "I have noticed that each day you walk into the woods. I wonder, why do you go there?" Moshe responded by telling the rabbi that he goes into the woods to find God. The rabbi replied gently, "That is a very good thing. I am glad that you are searching for God, but don't you know that God is the same everywhere?" Now Moshe looked at the rabbi and smiled, "Yes, but I am not."

Activity 3

The Balancing Act—*Keva* vs. *Kavanah*

Materials

- Copies of *The Way Into Jewish Prayer*

Procedure

1. Review the section on "Prayer as Art" on pages 33–37 in *The Way Into Jewish Prayer.* Talk about the balance between *keva* and *kavanah.*
   [Teacher's Tip: The importance that structure has in our service, but the necessity for our deep spiritual connection to prayer.]
2. Ask students to discuss *keva* vs. *kavanah* in their lives:
   a. How could you create a balance between the two?
   b. Does the synagogue play a role? If so, what?
   c. Do you feel you achieve *kavanah* during any of your prayer time?
      i. Is that dependent on you or things surrounding you in the congregation?
   d. Describe your experience of *kavanah:* Is it difficult? Frightening? Mystical? Freeing? Something else?
   e. Do the services you attend allow for both *keva* and *kavanah*?
   f. Do you think your fellow congregants experience *kavanah*?
   [Teacher's Tip: Heschel claims that too often there is spiritual absenteeism, "Some modern men and women pray by proxy, letting the rabbi or cantor do the work while they sit passively in their pews turning the pages; others read the words, but they recite the prayer book as if it were last week's newspaper.... The words are there but the souls who are to feel their meaning, to absorb their significance, are absent. They utter shells of syllables but put nothing of themselves into the shells" (p. 34–35).]

Wrap-up

Jewish prayer is a mix of fixed liturgy and spontaneous feeling. It requires discipline and sincerity. Our tradition says the best prayer uses both.

Activity 4

The Bedtime *Sh'ma*

Materials

- **Copies of a traditional *siddur* for each student**
- **Copies of Hand-out III: The Bedtime *Sh'ma***

Procedure

1. Introduce the Bedtime *Sh'ma* as something that is composed of both *keva* and *kavanah*.
2. Go through Hand-out III with students, reading aloud and discussing each item.
3. When you get to the section on the order of the bedtime prayers, turn to the proper page in the *siddurim* you are using and allow students to read through the prayers.
4. After reading through the prayers, discuss these questions with your students:
   a. Why do you think these prayers were chosen to read prior to going to sleep?
   b. Do you think it makes sense to include them all? Why or why not?
   c. Do you think there are other important topics that are missing from the traditional liturgy? If so, what might those be?
      [Teacher's Tip: Are they because we live in modern times?]
   d. If you do say these prayers now before bedtime, which one speaks to you the most and why? If not, could you see saying any of them? Why or why not?
5. Discuss bedtime rituals with your students and answer the following questions:
   a. What might ending the day with the Bedtime *Sh'ma* do for you?
   b. Do you have a bedtime ritual already in place?
   c. If you decided to say the *Sh'ma* at bedtime, what impact might that have on your life?
   d. If you decide not to recite the *Sh'ma*, are there other ways to ritualize the end of your day? *[Teacher's Tip: Other adult rituals might be to internally reflect on your day, or talk about the favorite part of your day with someone who is close to you.]*

Wrap-up

Sleep has fascinated the Jewish people throughout our history. The Bedtime *Sh'ma* was canonized to address it. Like other rubrics of prayer, it too is made up of both *keva* (fixed liturgy) and *kavanah* (spontaneity). Even today, marking the end of our day with prayer can be significant. We all have routines that we practice before we go to sleep. Ritualizing them in sacred ways can give equally sacred meaning to the end of our day.

Hand-out III

The Bedtime *Sh'ma*

Jewish Thoughts on Sleep

- Rabbi Yehoshua of Sachnin said in the name of Rabbi Levi, "The beginning of a man's downfall is sleep. Being asleep, he does not engage in study and does no work" (*Genesis Rabbah* 17:5).
- Rambam believes that the average person needs eight hours of sleep.
- If you use your daytime well, doing the *mitzvot* of God and serving God, then your hours of sleep are still considered a time of learning and doing *mitzvot.*
- Sleep is one-sixtieth of death (*Berachot* 57b).
- God gave us the gift of sleep so we could be refreshed each morning.
- The prayers said at night act as our nighttime guardian.

Kri'at Sh'ma al HaMitah (Liturgy)

Seder of a Traditional Service:

- *HaMapil* (the blessing over sleep)
- *Sh'ma*
- Psalms 91 and 3
- *Hashkiveinu*
- Verses from Genesis, Exodus, Zechariah, Song of Solomon, and Numbers; and Prayers for Protection at Night
- Psalm 128
- *Adon Olam*

Reform Movement Liturgy

- *HaMapil*
- *Sh'ma*
- *Hashkiveinu*
- Prayers for Protection at Night

Traditional Law Code on *Kri'at Sh'ma al HaMitah*

- "Just as [at the time of] rising, the recital of *Sh'ma* is next to [rising from] bed, so also [at the time of] lying down, recital of *Sh'ma* must be next to [getting into] bed" (*Berachot* 4b).
- "R. Joshua b. Levi says: Even if someone has recited the *Sh'ma* in the synagogue, it is a religious act to recite it again upon his or her bed" (*Berachot* 4b).
- "R. Isaac says: If one recites the *Sh'ma* upon his bed, it is as though he held a two-edged sword in his hand.... If one recites the *Sh'ma* upon his bed, the demons keep away from him" (*Berachot* 5a, derived from Psalm 149:5–6).
- Reciting *Sh'ma* and *HaMapil* each night applies to both men and women. It is especially important for someone who is sick, someone who recently gave birth, a bride, a groom, a mourner, and a Torah scholar, because they need extra protection (*Berachot* 54b).
- On the night of the Passover Seder one recites only the *Sh'ma* and *HaMapil* because on this night God guarantees protection (Mishnah).

Session III

The Synagogue Sanctuary: What's What and Why It Is So

Set Induction

Have students answer the following questions on a piece of paper:

1. Describe the sanctuary in your synagogue.
2. What makes your sanctuary unique?
3. Do you feel comfortable praying in your sanctuary?
4. Is there something you wish was different about your sanctuary?

Introduction to Lesson

"The beginning of communal prayer, however, is comfort in the worship environment. That means knowing what to expect when you enter, and understanding the vocabulary that describes what goes on there" (p. 40).

"Synagogues are the focus of Jewish life because they are the communal sacred center: a holy place for a holy community bent on doing holy work, not the least of which is community prayer" (p. 45).

Activity 1

Service of the Heart Replaces Sacrifice

Materials

- Copies of *The Way Into Jewish Prayer*
- Copies of the *Tanach*

Procedure

1. Ask for volunteers to read aloud "Service of the Heart Replaces Sacrifice," on pages 51–53 of *The Way Into Jewish Prayer* (skip the text piece on the bottom of page 51).

2. Talk about early biblical descriptions of sacrifice.
   [Teacher's Tip: Look at the following biblical references: Genesis 4:1–5, Genesis 8:20–22, and Genesis 22:1–8.]
3. Read aloud to the group the text on sacrifice at the bottom of page 51 of *The Way Into Jewish Prayer.*
4. Discuss the following questions:
   a. Do you think prayer is an adequate replacement for sacrifice?
   b. If prayer requires you to serve God with all your heart, can you do that if the prayer is only fixed *(keva)*? Or is *kavanah* required?
   c. What do you think was the purpose of sacrifice then? How has that changed? What is the purpose of prayer? Do they serve the same function?
   d. The text mentions facing east toward Jerusalem to pray. Is your sanctuary set up this way? Do you feel drawn to pray toward Jerusalem? Why or why not?

Wrap-up

When the Temple was destroyed, sacrifice ceased. It was replaced by the service of the heart, otherwise known as prayer. Now in order to communicate with God, we do not sacrifice our cattle; rather we search deep within ourselves and express ourselves through words, rituals, and emotions. Many of our congregations still recognize the original location of the Temple as being a significant and spiritual home. Others find it important to the Land and even to the State of Israel. For these reasons, many synagogues are built facing east toward Jerusalem.

Activity 2

The Ark

Advance Preparation

Teachers should take time prior to class to visit their synagogue library and find pictures of what the tabernacle/ark was believed to have looked like. Make copies and bring copies to class.

Materials

- **Books with pictures of what the tabernacle/ark was thought to have looked like**
  [Teacher's Tip: Use your local synagogue library. One place to look is Encyclopedia Judaica*; another is the volume on Exodus in the Jewish Publication Society's* Bible *series.]*
- **White paper**
- **Pencils/pens**
- **Markers/crayons**
- **Copies of *The Way Into Jewish Prayer***

Procedure

1. Talk about the ark with the students. Use pages 58–63 in *The Way Into Jewish Prayer* as your reference guide.
   [Teacher's Tip: Walk your students through this section, talking about what the ark was, its biblical roots, and what it has become today. While talking about the biblical account, it would be a good time to pass the pictures around.]
2. Ask for volunteers to read the text from Exodus on pages 59–60 of *The Way Into Jewish Prayer*.
3. Discuss the following questions:
   a. Why might God have put so much thought into how the ark should be made?
   b. Is the ark a focal point in your sanctuary? Is there something on it that makes it unique? Is there a part of it that is reminiscent of the ark God commanded Moses to build?
4. Pass out pieces of paper and ask students to draw an ark they feel would be appropriate for a sanctuary, taking into account what they have learned today, and what their own synagogue ark looks like.

Wrap-up

In the Torah, we have an account of God commanding the people to create a tabernacle in the desert. From that description, numerous drawings of what the tabernacle might have looked like have been created. Although the designs of today's sanctuaries might not reflect the design of the one in the Torah, the holiness and uniqueness of the biblical account lives on in what we build today.

Activity 3
The Torah Scrolls

Advance Preparation

Teacher needs to arrange access to a Torah for this activity.

Materials

- Torah
- Copies of *The Way Into Jewish Prayer*

Procedure

1. Talk about the Torah scroll using pages 63–67 of *The Way Into Jewish Prayer* as a guide.
   [Teacher's Tip: Emphasize such points as: How many books are in the Torah and what are they? When do we read the Torah? How does the scribe write the Torah? What goes on the Torah when it is in the ark?]

2. Take students into the sanctuary and take out the Torah, talking about each piece as you undress it.
   [Teacher's Tip: Talk about the crowns, the breastplate, and the yad. *See pages 65–66 of* The Way Into Jewish Prayer *for descriptions.]*
3. While the Torah is on the *bimah*, show the students all the special components that are found in the scroll.
   [Teacher's Tip: For example, the break between books, the Ten Commandments, the Song of the Sea, and how one might go about looking for a weekly Torah portion. Let the class work with the Torah scroll. Too often adults have never been close to it and find it intimidating.]
4. Have the students sit closely next to each other on the floor and unroll the Torah scroll (being careful that it does not touch the floor and they do not touch the writing with their fingers) so that each one of them has a section in their lap. Talk to them about the specific piece of text that is in front of them.

Wrap-up

The Jews are often called "The People of the Book." The Torah is our book. Not only is it the focal point of our sanctuary, it is also an integral part of our prayer services. The Torah is filled with our tradition's stories and we have a responsibility to treat it properly and with honor.

Session IV

The Community at Prayer: Who's Who and What They Do

Set Induction

Have students answer the following questions on a piece of paper:

1. What importance does your Jewish community have to you?
2. Have your most meaningful prayer experiences happened in a community or individually?
3. In your time of need, has your Jewish community been there to support you?

Introduction to Lesson

"The Jewish ideal of a prayerful person is someone who prays personally, privately, and passionately—but especially publicly" (p. 75).

Activity 1

Meet Your Clergy

Advance Preparation

Teachers should set a time during class in which the clergy team of the congregation can come and talk with students.

Materials

- Lined paper
- Pencils/pens
- List of the synagogue's clergy members and their titles

Procedure

1. Using pages 78–81 from *The Way Into Jewish Prayer* as a guide, talk about the role clergy plays in the synagogue.

[Teacher's Tip: Use the following questions to help guide the discussion: When did prayer leaders begin to be given the title "rabbi"? What is the purpose of the titles given to clergy today? How are priests and Levites honored? Who else is honored today and how? Who can or cannot lead prayer?]

2. Ask the students to write down questions they have always wanted to ask their clergy members but have not.
3. Invite your synagogue's clergy team to visit the class. Ask them to talk about their personal journey to their profession and the role they play within the synagogue structure. Allow time for students to ask their questions.

Wrap-up

The role of the clergy in today's synagogue is multi-faceted: leading services, counseling congregants, teaching, administrative work, life-cycle events, study, and more.

Activity 2

The Reform Movement Over Time

Note: The Reform Movement in America dates back to the middle of the nineteenth century. Since it provides several platforms of its beliefs through time, it is a particularly rich source of American Jewish history. In this activity, Reform Jews can see how their prayers reflect their beliefs. Jews of other denominations may note where their beliefs vary, and how their prayers demonstrate their differences.

Materials

- **Copies of the four major platforms in the Reform Movement (1885 Pittsburgh Conference, Columbus 1937, San Francisco 1976, and Pittsburgh Convention 1999)**
  [Teacher's Tip: This information can be downloaded at http://ccarnet.org.]
- **Pencils/pens**

Procedure

1. Introduce the four major Reform Movement platforms, each one an index of Reform Jewish belief: 1885 Pittsburgh Conference, Columbus 1937, San Francisco 1976, and Pittsburgh Convention 1999.
   [Teacher's Tip: Three of the main topics that each convention has tackled are the Reform views of God, Israel, and Torah. These three topics are often pictured as a triangle, with God, Israel, and Torah at its three corners.]
2. Split the class into four groups and assign each group a platform. Ask students to read through their platform, concentrating on what they say about God, Israel, and Torah. Each group should be prepared to come back together and report their findings.
3. Bring the group back together and review what each platform says.
4. Discuss with students:
   a. Why the changes?
   b. Are the changes evident at your synagogue?

c. Is your synagogue old enough to have gone through these changes too? If so, how were these changes enacted?

Wrap-up

Through these platforms you can see the development of thought in the Reform Movement in the United States. When it began, acculturation in America was most important. Over time, a shift occurred. The Reform Movement has appropriated tradition, embraced Israel, and emphasized change. What parallel changes do you see in other movements particularly (if you are not a Reform Jew) your own?

Activity 3

Torah Reading and *Aliyah*

Materials

- Copies of *siddurim* with the blessings for before and after the Torah reading
- Copies of *The Way Into Jewish Prayer*

Procedure

1. Talk about the Torah reading, *aliyahs,* and other acts associated with the Torah service. Use pages 98–102 in *The Way Into Jewish Prayer* as a guide.
   [Teacher's Tip: Use the following questions to help guide the discussion: Why is reading the Torah so central? What does the Torah reading symbolize?]
2. Pass out *siddurim* and turn to the page with the blessings that are said before and after the Torah reading. Ask for student volunteers to read the Hebrew and/or English aloud.
   Discuss with students:
   a. Have you ever been called for an *aliyah*? If so, how do you feel when doing it? Who gets called in your congregation and why?
3. If they do not know them, teach students the blessings in Hebrew.
4. Discuss the way a Torah service is conducted. Have various students do the different parts, assigning someone to read the Torah. Discuss the symbolism of each part.

Wrap-up

Reading the Torah is a *mitzvah*. There are also certain things that happen during the Torah service including: a *hakafah* (parade with the Torah), *aliyot* (blessings before and after the reading), and *hagbah* (having someone lift the Torah up high for all to see).

SESSION V

The Ideas of Jewish Prayer: What Matters Most

Set Induction

Have students answer the following questions on a piece of paper:

1. What role do you see women having in Judaism?
2. Does ritual permeate your life? Why or why not?
3. Can you describe any of the main ideas found in the prayer book?

Introduction to Lesson

"Ideas matter. Traditionally, the synagogue has been a place where people go to discover such ideas, which come not just from study, lectures, and sermons but from the very act of prayer" (p. 103).

Activity 1

Modern Rituals

Advance Preparation

Teachers should search the library, the Internet, and ask their clergy for modern rituals that their students might not have heard about.

Materials

- Prayer books
- Copies of modern rituals your congregation does or that you have compiled from Internet sites such as www.ritualwell.org
- Lined paper
- Pencils/pens
- Copies of *The Way Into Jewish Prayer*

Procedure

1. Talk to students about ritual's role in Judaism using pages 103–105 of *The Way Into Jewish Prayer* as a guide.
   [Teacher's Tip: Use the following questions to help guide discussion: What do you think about ritual? What does The Way Into Jewish Prayer *propose about ritual? Do you believe that ritual adds value to your prayer services? How is ritual used in your prayer services?]*
2. Discuss how ritual is used today and how it is constantly being re-invented to coincide with the times and what is going on in people's personal lives.
   [Teacher's Tip: There are some rituals that remain constant and others that are ever changing and even others that are being created. Jews are constantly being affected by new phenomena in their lives, and in search of ritualized ways of marking them. Rituals exist for widows who are remarrying, families that are moving into new homes, adoption, menopause, and becoming empty nesters, just to name a few.]
3. Pass out copies of new rituals and go through them. Discuss with students:
   a. What is surprising about them?
   b. What do you like/dislike?
   c. Have you ever been part of any of those rituals before?
   d. Do you sanctify transitions of choice?
4. Ask the students to think about an event in their lives they wished they could have marked with ritual. Ask them to spend some time creating a ritual that might work for that specific time.

Wrap-up

"Most people do not describe ritual [as important]. They think of it as mere pomp and circumstance, outer trappings, the fluff of religious life as opposed to the nuts and bolts of belief that give a religion substance. But good ritual is all about ideas that move us" (pp. 103–104). Hopefully this activity has introduced you to new rituals and has helped you think about different ways in which rituals can affect your life.

Activity 2
Prayer Books for Women

Materials

- Copies of *The Way Into Jewish Prayer*

Procedure

1. Talk about the prayer books for women that once existed, using pages 105–108 of *The Way Into Jewish Prayer* as a guide.
   [Teacher's Tip: Use the following questions to help guide the discussion: What roles of women were once taken for granted? How do you feel about the roles women had? Have women's roles changed today?]
2. Read aloud the prayers that are included in *The Way Into Jewish Prayer* for baking *challah*, hoping to become pregnant, departure for errands, and the *midrash* on lighting Shabbat candles.
3. Discuss the following questions:
   a. What are your initial reactions to these pieces?
   b. Do you believe that specific prayers should still exist just for women or for men?
   c. Is there something comforting and familiar about the gender specific prayers, or should prayers that address men and women simply be treated equally?
   d. If you are a woman, do you feel you have an equal place in Judaism? Are you satisfied with the roles women play in Judaism?
   e. All movements struggle with making liturgy, rituals, and Jewish life in general accessible to women. What is your movement doing? Is it sufficient?

Wrap-up

There has been a development of women's roles in Judaism over time. From these pages, we see how certain eras created special prayer books for women, sometimes addressing issues directly relevant to women's lives. But women were never central to Jewish communal consciousness. That is changing in our time. Women now are often rabbis, cantors, educators, synagogue administrators, and lay leaders. They often still wish to have rituals addressed to the uniqueness of women's lives. The same, however, may also be true for men. The desire to mark specific times in the lives of everyone seems to be as vital as ever.

Activity 3

Four Kinds of Prayer Ideas

Materials

- **Copies of Hand-out IV: Four Kinds of Prayer Ideas Text Sheet**
- **Prayer books**
- **Copies of *The Way Into Jewish Prayer***

Procedure

1. Talk about the four different types of prayer book ideas (Theology, Anthropology, Cosmology, and Eschatology). Go through their definitions and talk briefly about each idea. *[Teacher's Tip: For definitions of these ideas see pages 108–133 of* The Way Into Jewish Prayer. *Use the following questions to guide the discussion: Describe what you think is the idea behind each prayer? When do these ideas come out during the prayer service? Are you cognizant of them? Which idea or ideas are you most drawn to and why? What is the history of these ideas as the book presents it?]*
2. Pass out the text sheet that has an example of the different type of text that fits into each category.
3. Go through each text and talk about what makes it fit into a specific prayer book idea.
4. Pass out prayer books and put the students in pairs. Ask them to go through the prayer book and come up with another prayer that would fit each category.
5. Have them come back together and share what they discovered with the group.

Wrap-up

There are four main prayer ideas found in our tradition: Theology, Anthropology, Cosmology, and Eschatology. Each idea is evident in a range of texts from our tradition. All of them combined make our prayer service of today.

Hand-out IV

Four Kinds of Prayer Ideas Text Sheet

Theology

Definition: The doctrine of God.
Text: Psalm 23:1–4

> The Lord is my shepherd,
>
> I shall not want.
>
> He maketh me lie down in green pastures.
>
> He leadeth me beside the still waters.
>
> He restoreth my soul.
>
> He guideth me in straight paths for his name's sake.
>
> Yea, though I walk through the valley of the shadow of death
>
> I will fear no evil,
>
> For thou art with me.
>
> Thy rod and thy staff, they comfort me.

Anthropology

Definition: The religious doctrine of human nature.
Text: Talmud, *Berachot* 17a

> I am God's creature and others are God's creatures. My work is in town, theirs in the country; I rise early to do my work, they rise early for theirs. They do not presume to do my work and I do not presume to do theirs. Can you say that I do much and they do less? We have learned, one may do little or a lot; it is all the same as long as we direct our heart to heaven.

Cosmology

Definition: What we think the world is like.
Text: Taken from *Gates of Prayer*

> Days pass and the years vanish, and we walk sightless among miracles. Adonai, fill our eyes with seeing and our minds with knowing; let there be moments when the lightning of Your Presence illumines the darkness in which we walk. Help us to see, wherever we gaze, that the bush burns unconsumed. And we, clay touched by God, will reach out for holiness, and exclaim in wonder: How filled with awe is this place, and we did not know it!

Eschatology

Definition: The doctrine of the end of time.
Text: Talmud, Bereshit 17a

> In the world to come, there will be no eating, no drinking, no sexual intercourse, no business, no jealousy, no hatred, and no competition. Instead, the righteous will sit with crowns on their heads, feasting on the luminosity of the divine presence.

Text: Talmud, *Berachot* 17a

> Rav said: The World to Come is not like this world, In the world to come there is no eating, no drinking, no sexual intercourse, no business, no jealousy, no hatred and no rivalry. Instead, the righteous sit with crowns on their heads and delight in the luminosity of the Divine Presence, as it said: "they gazed at God, and they ate and drank" (Exodus 24:11).

Session VI

A Prayerful Person at Home and on the Way: When the Ordinary Can Be Sacred

Set Induction

Have students answer the following questions on a piece of paper:

1. When do you feel most prayerful?
2. How do you make your day, week, year Jewish?
3. Do you believe that prayers should be said both inside and outside of the synagogue? Why or why not?

Introduction to Lesson

"'Everyone should say one hundred blessings daily,'" said Rabbi Meir ... Rabbi Meir was emphasizing ... the delightful spontaneity of prayer that is evoked from the certain knowledge that, as the Talmud puts it, the Gates of Heaven are always open" (p. 135).

Activity 1

What Is a Blessing?

Materials

- Text sheet with blessings for things found in the natural world
- Copies of *The Way Into Jewish Prayer*

Procedure

1. Define what constitutes a blessing. Discuss the different types of blessing found in our liturgy.
   [Teacher's Tip: Note especially the short blessings that people know by heart (like Hamotzi*), they are "one-line expressions of praise for God, evoked by recognition of the sacred, often within the ordinary" (p. 135).]*

2. Discuss with students:
    a. Why do you say blessings?
    b. What importance can blessings add to your life?
    c. Do you ever say blessings outside of the synagogue? If so, which ones?
    d. Have you ever created your own blessing over something? If so, what?
    e. How many blessings do you really say?
    f. What do Jews traditionally say blessings over?
3. Pass out a list with blessings over different things one might find in nature and discuss each item.

Wrap-up

There are many times in our lives when saying a blessing can make the ordinary, extraordinary. By going through the examples we studied, we can now see that Judaism is uniquely outfitted to do that. Many blessings already exist for things that we come across in our everyday lives, but holiness can always be found as well in original spontaneous prayer.

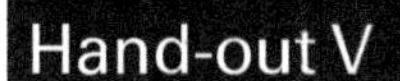

Blessings to Recite over Natural Things

The blessing to say...

Upon seeing lightning, shooting stars, high mountains, or a sunrise...
Blessed are You, Adonai our God, Ruler of the universe, Who makes the works of creation.

Upon hearing thunder or seeing a storm...
Blessed are You, Adonai our God, Ruler of the universe, Whose strength and power fill the universe.

Upon seeing exceptionally beautiful creatures...
Blessed are You, Adonai our God, Ruler of the universe, that there are such as this in God's world.

Upon smelling fragrant trees or shrubs...
Blessed are You, Adonai our God, Ruler of the universe, Who creates fragrant trees.

Upon seeing the ocean...
Blessed are You, Adonai our God, Ruler of the universe, Who has made the great sea.

Activity 2
Sacred Time

Advance Preparation

Teachers should ask clergy members or educators for copies of the Jewish calendar. Calendars are often available in local stores right before Rosh Hashanah. Synagogues often have their own calendar version of the holidays and candle lightings available. Educators sometimes have an artwork version.

Materials

- Copies of a Jewish calendar
- Copies of *The Way Into Jewish Prayer*

Procedure

1. Introduce the concept of the Jewish calendar.
   [Teacher's Tip: Where it came from. Why we have it. Differences between it and a secular calendar.]
2. Talk about the Jewish calendar as sacred time.
   [Teacher's Tip: "There is Jewish time, therefore the time of the year sensed in Jewish bones and minds.... The calendar has its way upon our souls" (p. 152).]
3. Pass out copies of the Jewish calendar and go through it with students. Look at where the holidays fall.
   a. What is important about those seasons?
   b. How can we transpose this calendar onto our secular calendar?
4. Talk about the emotions that particular holidays evoke and how Judaism accounts for that in their placement.
   [Teacher's Tip: Examples of this are: Sukkot—the harvest holiday that falls appropriately during one of the harvest times of the year, when the leaves are changing. One of the themes of Passover is rebirth and it falls right at the time of year where flowers begin to bloom and trees begin to grow leaves.]
5. Divide students into pairs and have them share what their favorite Jewish holidays are and why. Have them relate their choice to topics already discussed (e.g., sacred space or blessings) in *The Way Into Jewish Prayer* thus far.
   [Teacher's Tip: For example, a student might like Sukkot because of the sacred space (sukkah) or because of the blessings you say over the lulav *and* etrog.*]*
6. After the students are finished, have them share what they have discussed with the class.

Wrap-up

The Jewish calendar is exceptional. It forces us to rethink our year through a different lens. "It adds texture to time, preventing the days of the year from being all the same. In so doing, it also provides a stunning variety of fasts and feasts, all of which together evoke an equal variation of mood and emotions, thus making us more deeply human" (p. 153).

Activity 3

Thank You for the Gift of Food

Advance Preparation

Teachers should go through the list of food items and bring a sampling of food items to class that fits into each *b'racha,* so the students can say the blessing and then eat the food.

Materials

- Copies of Hand-out VI: Choosing the Correct *B'racha*
- Copies of Hand-out VII: Food *B'rachot*
- A sampling of food that fits into each category
- Copies of *Birkat haMazon* (Grace after the Meal)
- Copies of *The Way Into Jewish Prayer*

Procedure

1. Talk about the many blessings we have over food and why that might be important, using pages 136–141 in *The Way Into Jewish Prayer* as a guide. Ask if anyone says the blessings over food regularly. If so, ask them to talk about what it feels like to do so.
2. Pass out Hand-outs VI and VII, the *b'racha* sheets, and go through the order with students.
3. Put a number of different foods in the center of the table. Ask each person to take one of everything. Before anything is eaten, ask a student in the class to say the proper blessing over the item of food. Continue doing so until each item is blessed.
4. Talk about bringing this idea home. Review the list of foods and their proper blessings.
   a. How can you incorporate this into your family structure?
5. Conclude with discussion of the *Birkat haMazon* and recite the blessing together with students.

Wrap-up

Before and after every meal, Judaism provides blessings that express appreciation for the food, the company, and the ability to reach each day.

Hand-out VI

Choosing the Correct *B'racha*

As a general rule, the most specific *b'racha* possible should be said for any food item. Among other things, specific blessings allow us to focus more directly on whatever it is that we are grateful for.

Baruch ata Adonai, Eloheinu melech ha'olam...
Blessed are You, Adonai our God, Ruler of the universe, Who...

Borei pree hagafen.
creates the fruit of the vine.

Hamotzi lechem min ha'aretz
brings forth bread from the earth.

Borei pree ha'eitz.
creates the fruit of the tree.

Borei meenei m'zonot.
creates various kinds of food.

Borei pree ha'adama.
creates the fruit of the earth.

Shehakol neeh'yeh bidvaro.
by whose words all things come into being.

Hand-out VII

Food *B'rachot*

Apple	*ha'eitz*	Lettuce	*ha'adama*
Avocado	*ha'eitz*	Mac & Cheese	*m'zonot*
Banana	*ha'adama*	Meat	*shehakol*
Blueberries	*ha'eitz*	Milk	*shehakol*
Pretzel	*m'zonot*	Milkshake	*shehakol*
Bread	*ha'motzi*	Muffins	*m'zonot*
Cake	*m'zonot*	Orange	*ha'eitz*
Candy	*shehakol*	Pasta	*m'zonot*
Carrot	*ha'adama*	Peach	*ha'eitz*
Challah	*ha'motzi*	Peanut Butter	*shehakol*
Cheese	*shehakol*	Peanuts	*ha'adama*
Cherry	*ha'eitz*	Pear	*ha'eitz*
Chocolate	*shehakol*	Pineapple	*ha'adama*
Cookies	*m'zonot*	Pizza	*ha'motzi*
Corn	*ha'adama*	Popsicle	*shehakol*
Corn flakes	*ha'adama*	Potato	*ha'adama*
Cucumber	*ha'adama*	Raisins	*ha'eitz*
Cupcake	*m'zonot*	Raisin Bran	*m'zonot*
Eggs	*shehakol*	Strawberry	*ha'eitz*
Fish	*shehakol*	Tomatoes	*ha'adama*
French fries	*ha'adama*	Waffles	*m'zonot*
Grapes	*shehakol*	Water	*shehakol*
Juice	*shehakol*	Watermelon	*ha'adama*

Additional Readings

Benstein, Jeremy. *The Way Into Judaism and the Environment.* Woodstock, VT: Jewish Lights, 2006.

Cohen, Norman. *The Way Into Torah.* Woodstock, VT: Jewish Lights, 2004.

Dardashti, Danielle, and Roni Sarig. *The Jewish Lights Book of Fun Classroom Activities: Simple and Seasonal Projects for Teachers and Students.* Woodstock, VT: Jewish Lights, 2004.

Dorff, Elliot. *The Way Into* Tikkun Olam *(Repairing the World).* Woodstock, VT: Jewish Lights, 2006.

Fishman, Sylvia Barack. *The Way Into the Varieties of Jewishness.* Woodstock, VT: Jewish Lights, 2007.

Gillman, Neil. *The Way Into Encountering God in Judaism.* Woodstock, VT: Jewish Lights, 2004.

Hoffman, Lawrence. "The Presence of God at Worship," in *The Art of Public Prayer: Not for Clergy Only.* Woodstock, VT: SkyLight Paths, 1999.

———. *The Canonization of the Synagogue Service.* Notre Dame, IN: University of Notre Dame Press, 1979.

———. *My People's Prayer Book: Traditional Prayers, Moderns Commentaries.* Vols. 1–10. Woodstock, VT: Jewish Lights, 2007–.

———. "Synagogues and American Spirituality," in Henry and Daniel Stolzman, *Synagogue Architecture in America: Faith, Spirit and Identity.* Australia: Image Publishing, 2004.

———. "Reconstructing Ritual as Identity and Culture" in Paul Bradshaw and Lawrence Hoffman, eds., *The Making of Christian and Jewish Worship:* 22–39. University of Notre Dame, 1991.

Kula, Irwin, and Vanessa L. Ochs, eds. *The Book of Jewish Sacred Practices: CLAL's Guide to Everyday and Holiday Rituals and Blessings.* Woodstock, VT: Jewish Lights, 2001.

Kushner, Lawrence. *The Way Into Jewish Mystical Tradition.* Woodstock, VT: Jewish Lights, 2000.

Petuchowski, Jakob. "Spontaneity and Tradition," in *Understanding Jewish Prayer*: 3–16. New York: KTAV, 1972.

Meyer, Michael. *Response to Modernity: A History of the Reform Movement in Judaism.* Detroit: Wayne State University Press, 1988.

Olitzky, Kerry M., and Daniel Judson. *The Rituals and Practices of a Jewish Life: A Handbook for Personal Spiritual Renewal.* Woodstock, VT: Jewish Lights, 2002.

Orenstein, Debra, ed. *Lifecycles, Vol. 1: Jewish Women on Life Passages and Personal Milestones.* Woodstock VT: Jewish Lights, 1994.

Orenstein, Debra, and Jane Rachel Litman, eds. *Lifecycles, Vol. 2: Jewish Women on Biblical Themes in Contemporary Life.* Woodstock, VT: Jewish Light, 1997.

Prager, Marcia. *The Path of Blessing: Experiencing the Energy and Abundance of the Divine.* Woodstock, VT: Jewish Lights, 2003.

Sonsino, Rifat. *The Many Faces of God.* New York: URJ Press, 2004

Washofsky, Mark. *Jewish Living: A Guide to Contemporary Reform Practice.* New York: UAHC Press, 2001.

Rabbi Jennifer Ossakow Goldsmith is director of Life Long Learning at Larchmont Temple in Larchmont, New York.

Rabbi Lawrence A. Hoffman, PhD, is the Stephen and Barbara Friedman Chair of Liturgy and Worship at Hebrew Union College–Jewish Institute of Religion, where he has served for more than three decades. A world-renowned liturgist, he has combined research in Jewish ritual, worship, and spirituality with a passion for the spiritual renewal of contemporary Judaism.

Hoffman has written and edited over twenty-five books, including *Rethinking Synagogues: A New Vocabulary for Congregational Life* (Jewish Lights), a finalist for the National Jewish Book Award; *The Art of Public Prayer: Not for Clergy Only* (SkyLight Paths), now used nationally by Jews and Christians as a handbook for liturgical planners in church and synagogue; as well as a revision of *What Is a Jew?*, the best-selling classic that remains the most widely read introduction to Judaism ever written in any language. He is the editor of the acclaimed multi-volume series *My People's Prayerbook: Traditional Prayers, Modern Commentaries* (Jewish Lights). He is also a founder of Synagogue 3000 (formerly synagogue 2000), a transdenominational project designed to transform synagogues into the moral and spiritual centers for the twenty-first century.